Thank you so much for choosing our activi
We truly hope that our book brings joy and

We would be honored if you could spare a moment to leave a review of our book. Your feedback is invaluable to us and helps us improve and reach more families in need of educational and entertaining resources.

Thank you again for choosing our activity book, and we can't wait to hear what you and your kids think!

This Book Belongs To

_____

_____

1

Welcome

To

The Ultimate Baseball Activity Book For Kids Ages 8-12!

Get ready for an action-packed journey into the world of baseball, filled with excitement and fun. This activity book is jam-packed with 85 thrilling baseball-themed activities, games, and puzzles that will keep you entertained for hours. From word searches and math challenges to designing your own team and crossword puzzles, this book has it all. So grab your bat, put on your glove, and dive into the world of baseball as you embark on an adventure of imagination, creativity, and endless enjoyment. Get ready to swing for the fences and have a grand slam of fun!

Are you ready? Let's go!

Word Search #1

Uncovering the hidden baseball terms in the grid by looking in all directions, including backwards and diagonally

```
C F S O E R Q I T R S G K A
Y U T S S P Z L N G P L V K
O G R N P I J Q U F D O I O
Q B I V W P B U F N I V H U
S I K Y E P C N O U P E N B
F D E W U B U M P I R E L T
U G O B Y R A A O E P L J D
G C U X E I K L H L A W K X
W D T M D N F C L B F Y U C
C S O Q R L T U T U S I L Q
L H T T W I B S G Q N C T R
H O M E P L A T E X O Q L N
T S X T A F Y R Y R V Y S D
L H P U R L X R G Z C N Q F
```

Steal	Home run	Diamond
Umpire	Fastball	Strikeout
Pitcher	Bullpen	Curveball
Infield	Glove	Home plate

Pitching Challenge Maze

Showcase your pitching skills as you aim for the catcher's mitt while outmaneuvering the batters

5

Dream Team Creation

Welcome to the exciting world of team ownership!

Get ready to unleash your creativity and imagination as you design your very own baseball team. This activity is divided into 9 steps, each allowing you to dive into a different aspect of team creation. From selecting a unique team name to designing jerseys, creating a team mascot, and even describing a home stadium, you'll have the opportunity to bring your dream team to life.

Throughout this activity, you'll embark on a journey of team ownership, where you'll make decisions that shape the identity of your team. Don't worry if you feel overwhelmed at any point – you can tackle each step at your own pace and come back to it later when you feel confident and inspired.

So, let's get started on this exciting adventure! Take each step with enthusiasm and embrace the joy of building your dream baseball team.

Step 1: Name and Logo Creation

Design a memorable name and logo for your baseball dream team and showcase your creativity and imagination

Team NAME

Team LOGO

Step 2: Jersey Design

Unleash your fashion sense! Design a unique and stylish jersey for your baseball dream team

Step 3: Home Stadium

The epicenter of victory! Describe the home stadium of your Baseball dream team

Step 4: Roster Creation

Building the dream team! Create a roster for your team, including positions and numbers for each player

Name	Position	Jersey Number

Step 5: Mascot Creation

Create a unique and energetic mascot for your team

Step 6: Team Description

Introduce your team to the world! Write a brief description highlighting your baseball team's name, home stadium, strengths, playing style, and what makes them unique.

Step 7: Cap Design

Step into the world of custom cap design and elevate your team's style on the field!

Step 8: Ticket Design

Get your tickets ready! Design an eye-catching and professional ticket template for your team's games

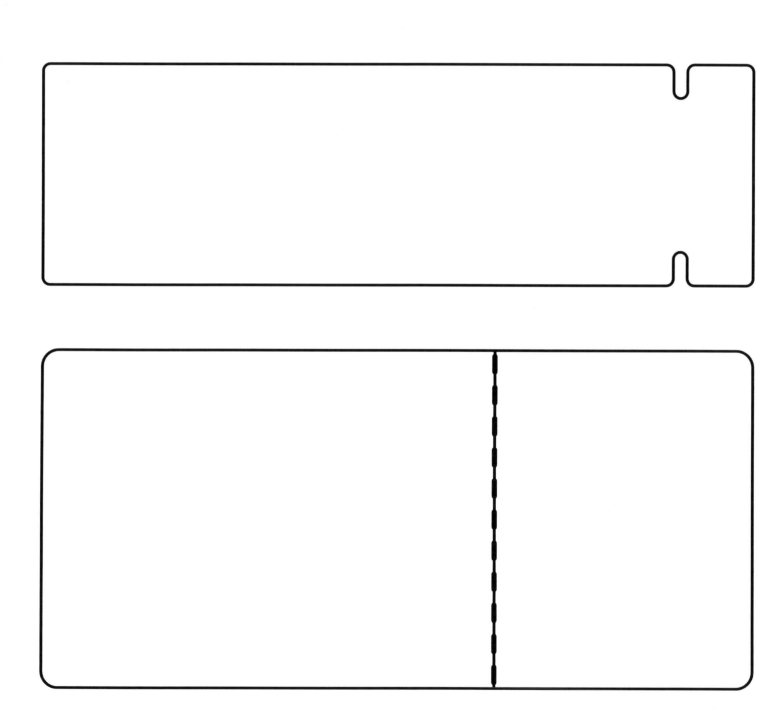

Step 9: Team Anthem

Fuel your team's spirit and propel your baseball team to victory with the power of music! Create an inspiring anthem or song that embodies the heart and soul of your team. Unleash your creativity as you craft lyrics that capture the enthusiasm, unity, and unyielding determination of your baseball dream team

Baseball Diamond

Identify and label the key elements of the baseball diamond and assign players to their positions

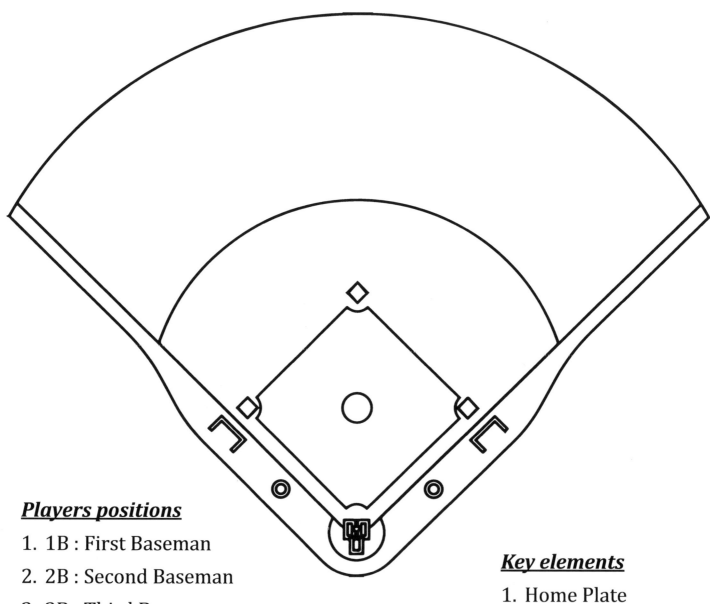

Players positions

1. 1B : First Baseman
2. 2B : Second Baseman
3. 3B : Third Baseman
4. SS : Shortstop
5. RF : Right Fielder
6. LF : Left Fielder
7. CF : Center Fielder
8. P : Pitcher
9. C : Catcher

Key elements

1. Home Plate
2. First Base
3. Second Base
4. Third Base
5. Pitcher's Mound
6. Baseline
7. Foul Line

Fun Baseball Facts

Baseball is believed to have originated from a game called "rounders" played in England in the 18th century.

The Baseball Hall of Fame, located in Cooperstown, New York, honors the greatest players, managers, and other contributors to the sport.

The first recorded baseball game took place in 1846 in Hoboken, New Jersey.

In baseball, it's extremely rare for one player to make all three outs by themselves. It's called an 'unassisted triple play' and has only happened 15 times in history

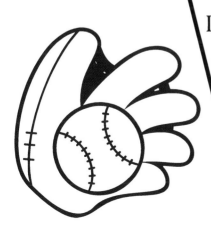

Drawing Activity

Put your artistic talents to use by replicating the image with your own drawing skills

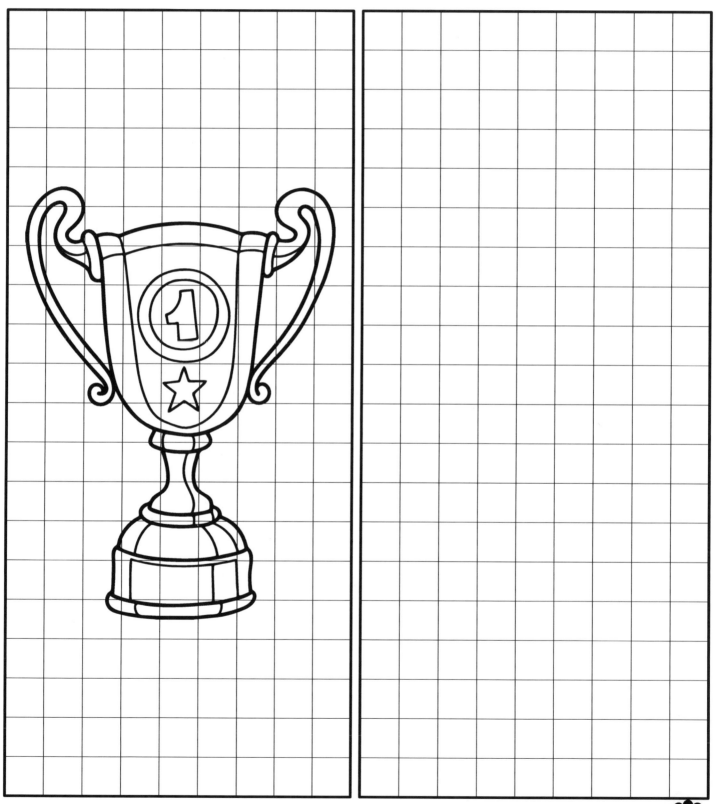

Math Meets Maze

Guide the pitcher to throw the ball by following the numbered path from 1 to 20. Can you make a perfect pitch and strike out the batter?

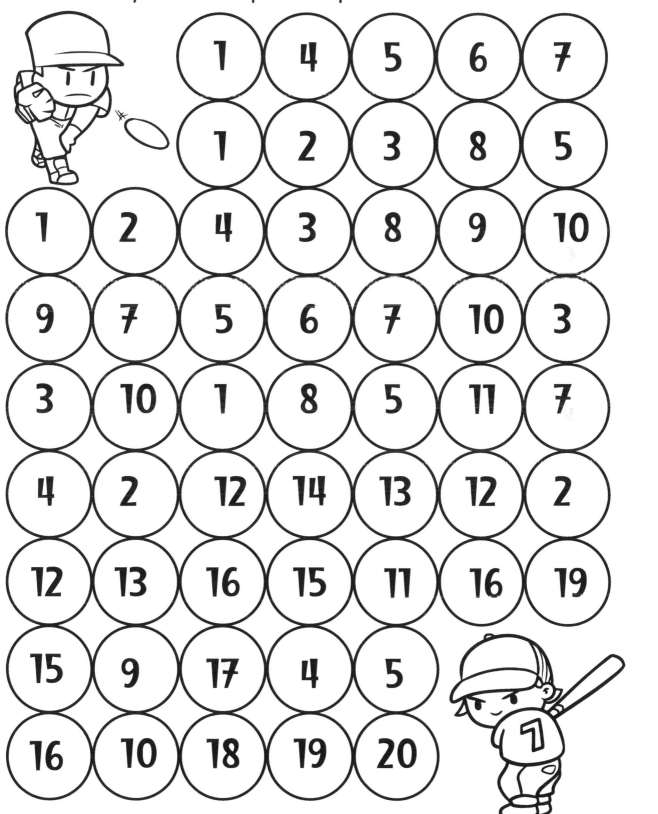

Decoding Baseball Jokes #1

Can you solve the secret code and uncover the hidden answer

a	b	d	e	f	h	i	j	l	m	n
1	2	3	4	5	6	7	8	9	10	11

o	p	r	s	t	u	w	y
12	13	14	15	16	17	18	19

Where does a baseball player go when he needs a new uniform?

11	4	18	8	4	14	15	4	19	

Where should a baseball player never wear red?

7	11	16	6	4	2	17	9	9	13	4	11

What do baseball players eat on?

6	12	10	4	13	9	1	16	4	15

Word Search #2

Uncovering the hidden baseball terms in the grid by looking in all directions, including backwards and diagonally

```
Y  B  A  C  A  T  C  H  E  R  S  M  I  T  T
J  P  L  N  I  P  E  Z  F  M  K  X  L  S  L
V  O  Y  Z  N  Y  N  T  U  B  C  W  F  P  E
E  P  G  F  K  O  B  G  P  Y  Q  G  A  R  F
X  B  K  C  H  R  U  O  N  D  E  C  K  I  T
F  N  F  P  O  N  T  N  Q  U  E  V  Y  N  F
W  W  E  Z  G  S  T  G  C  D  A  A  Y  G  I
U  B  A  T  T  I  N  G  H  E  L  M  E  T  E
B  V  K  R  D  Y  V  P  P  P  R  O  A  R  L
X  A  O  O  K  M  D  U  E  W  P  Q  P  A  D
Q  H  L  B  P  L  D  L  F  G  J  C  M  I  E
S  T  O  L  E  N  B  A  S  E  G  T  E  N  R
V  G  U  C  I  U  J  W  J  D  B  Q  S  I  Y
C  O  T  W  O  H  G  M  J  A  C  R  C  N  R
F  N  Z  D  I  I  Q  D  U  W  J  I  U  G  V
```

Stolen base	On deck	Double play
Announcer	Catcher's mitt	Windup
Ball	Left fielder	Spring training
Shortstop	Foul	Batting helmet

Players Anagram Challenge #1

Unscramble the names of the baseball greats and test your knowledge of the sport

WTLRAE NOHSJON

_ _ _ _ _ _ _ _ _ _ _ _ _ _ _ _ _ _

BEAB HRUT

_ _ _ _ _ _ _ _ _ _ _ _ _ _ _ _ _ _

WADNERW EMHUCNCT

_ _ _ _ _ _ _ _ _ _ _ _ _ _ _ _ _ _

IELILW YSEAM

_ _ _ _ _ _ _ _ _ _ _ _ _ _ _ _ _ _

EKIM TROUT

_ _ _ _ _ _ _ _ _ _ _ _ _ _ _ _ _ _

SONUH REWAGN

_ _ _ _ _ _ _ _ _ _ _ _ _ _ _ _ _ _

My Favorite Player Profile Card

Think you're a pro at knowing your favorite player? Prove it!

Name: _____

Position: _____

Team: _____

Jersey number: _____

Height: _____

Weight: _____

Age: _____

Nickname: _____

Hometown: _____

Batting/Throwing Hand:

_____

Image

Career Highlights

Awards: _____

_____

_____

_____

Championships: _____

_____

_____

_____

Other notable
accomplishments: _____

_____

_____

_____

_____

Career Statistics

Games played: _____

Batting Average: _____

Home Runs: _____

Hits: _____

Stolen Bases: _____

Strikeouts: _____

Memorable Baseball Moment

_____

_____

_____

Strike for Glory

Help the player make an unforgettable mark in history by scoring their first strike!

Acrostic Poem #1

An acrostic poem is a type of poem where the first letter of each line spells out a word or phrase. All lines should relate to or Describe the poem.
Write an acrostic poem for the word below

BASEBALL

B _

A _

S _

E _

B _

A _

L _

L _

Guess The Player #1

Put your skills to the test!
Can you identify the player from the clues given?

1. He was not only a great hitter but also a pitcher in his early career

2. This player's first name is George Herman, but he is more commonly known by his famous nickname.

3. When it came to home runs, this player had a knack for breaking records and sending the crowd into a frenzy!

4. He played during the "Roaring Twenties" and became a symbol of the era, capturing the imagination of fans across the country

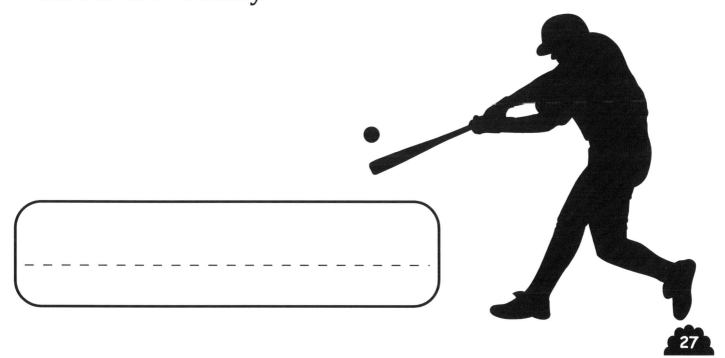

Crossword Game #1

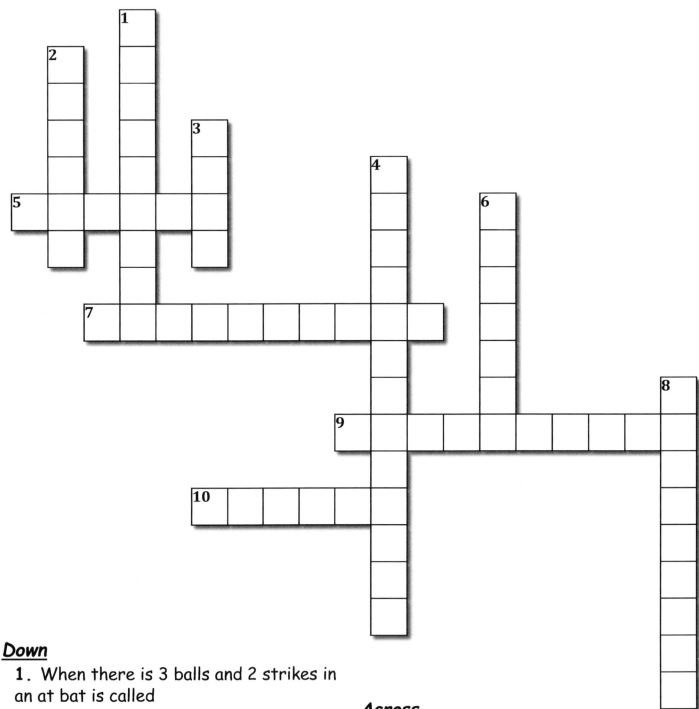

Down

1. When there is 3 balls and 2 strikes in an at bat is called

2. When you hit and you run to third base

3. You have to get three in these to get out of an inning

4. A fielder who covers the area between first and second base.

6. The player responsible for throwing the ball to the batter.

8. A homerun with 3 people on base

Across

5. When the ball is hit in the air and the defender catches it

7. The area in fair territory where the pitcher must deliver the ball.

9. When you are on base you are called a...

10. When you hit and run to second its called...

Connect the Dots #1

Join the fun! Connect the dots from 1 to 36 and discover the hidden picture

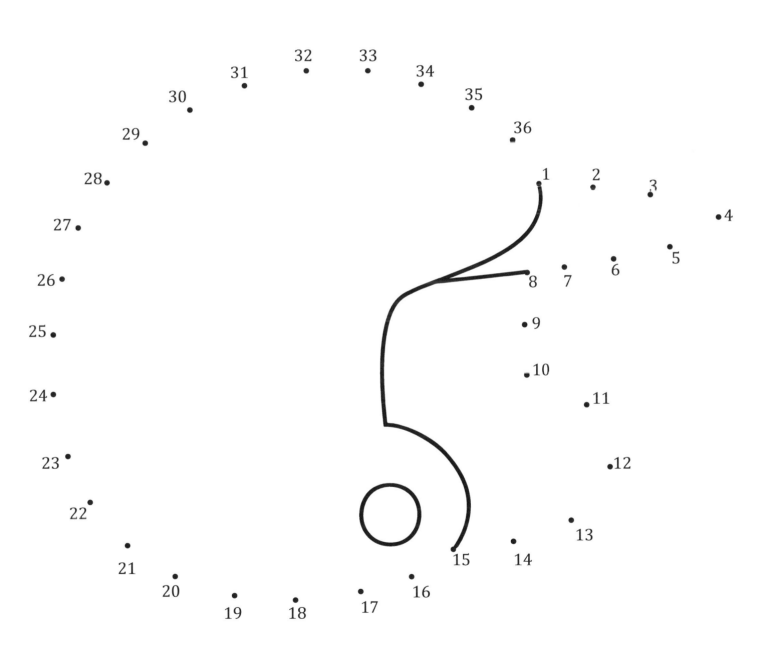

Baseball Commentary

Imagine you're a super cool announcer for a thrilling baseball game! Use exciting and vivid words to describe all the amazing things the players are doing on the field.
Get ready to add tons of excitement to your commentary!

Fun Baseball Facts

The oldest ballpark in baseball is Fenway Park, located in Boston. It has been welcoming fans since 1912

Did You Know?

Abner Doubleday was said to have invented baseball as it is today but most baseball historians do not support this claim.

A regulation baseball has exactly 108 stitches

The first official baseball game for the visually impaired was played in 1980, leading to the development of beep baseball, a modified version of the sport using sound-emitting balls.

Drawing Activity

Put your artistic talents to use by replicating the image with your own drawing skills

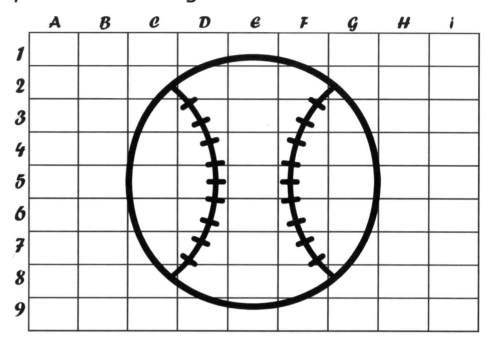

Baseball Math #1

Put your math skills to the test and find the value of each?

(glove) + (bat) = (helmet) + 1

(baseball) + (baseball) = (glove)

5 = (baseball) + (helmet)

(helmet) - 3 = 1

(glove) = ☐   (bat) = ☐   (helmet) = ☐

(baseball) = ☐

Baseball Scramble Game #1

Look at the letters around the picture.
Try to rearrange them to fill in the blanks

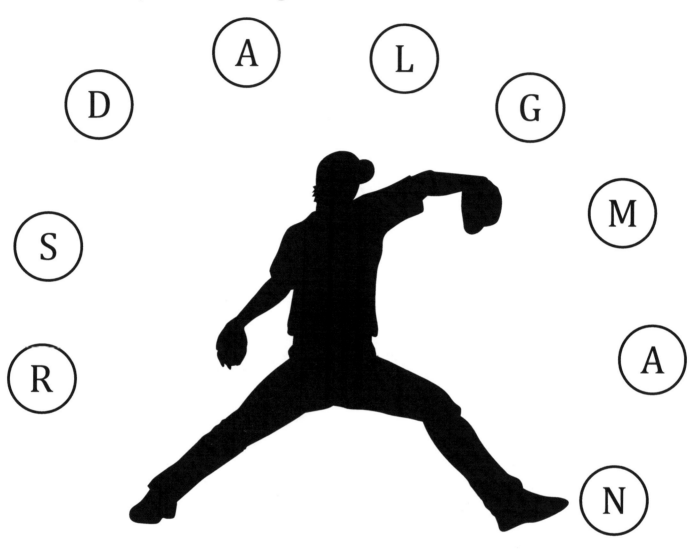

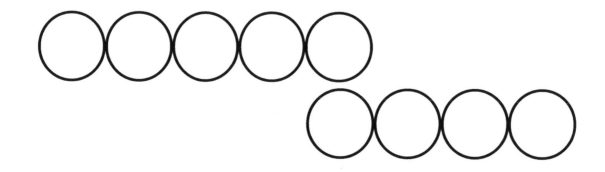

The Lost Bat

Uh-oh! The Batter has misplaced his trusty bat and he needs your awesome skills to help him track it down

Decoding Baseball Jokes #2

Can you solve the secret code and uncover the hidden answer

a	b	c	d	e	f	g	h	i	j	k	l	m
1	2	3	4	5	6	7	8	9	10	11	12	13

n	o	p	q	r	s	t	u	v	w	x	y	z
14	15	16	17	18	19	20	21	22	23	24	25	26

Why was the baseball player at the store?

6	15	18	1	19	1	12	5	19	16	9	20	3	8

What did the baseball glove say to the ball?

3	1	20	3	8	25	15	21	12	1	20	5	18

What do you call a baseball player who doesn't take a bath?

1	4	9	18	20	25	19	12	9	4	5	18

What's a baseball player's favorite type of music?

19	23	9	14	7

Word Search #3

Uncovering the hidden baseball terms in the grid by looking in all directions, including backwards and diagonally

```
A  K  O  S  C  S  X  I  G  E  F  T  P  I  P
O  U  T  F  I  E  L  D  R  V  B  V  E  P  B
P  H  R  B  I  C  E  K  A  D  O  D  L  A  O
X  E  I  W  B  O  S  H  N  G  I  Q  U  V  M
J  J  G  P  Z  N  V  A  D  L  H  F  M  C  V
H  T  H  I  R  D  B  A  S  E  M  A  N  W  E
U  H  T  B  M  B  V  Z  L  L  K  D  Q  I  K
A  I  F  O  Q  A  I  O  A  K  I  A  T  S  F
R  B  I  M  E  S  C  Y  M  D  B  D  J  S  P
H  R  E  G  K  E  F  U  U  O  U  T  I  V  K
F  T  L  H  O  M  U  R  T  U  O  E  N  N  L
G  D  D  M  P  A  P  A  Z  B  A  T  Q  W  G
M  B  E  H  Q  N  V  S  R  L  I  F  C  U  Q
F  I  R  M  C  A  T  C  H  E  R  M  K  M  S
N  J  J  X  W  H  I  E  F  Q  V  F  U  D  Y
```

Third baseman	Double	Sliding
Second baseman	Out	Slide
Right fielder	Bat	Team
Grand slam	Catcher	Outfield

My Favorite Baseball Team

Welcome to the exciting world of baseball team profiling! In this activity, you have the opportunity to create a comprehensive profile of your favorite baseball team. Get ready to dive into the rich history, key players, coaches, home stadium, and overall team description. Let your passion for the game shine as you showcase the essence of your beloved team in just three simple steps.

Are you ready to unlock the secrets and celebrate the greatness of your chosen team?

Step 1: Team Name and Logo

Show your team spirit by displaying the team's name / nickname and logo on the card

Team NAME and NICKNAME

Team LOGO

Step2: History & Key Players

Discover your team's most memorable moments in history and get to know the current and former stars that made them stand out

Team History

Key Players

Key Coaches

Step 3: Stadium & Description

Explore the home stadium and style of play of your team, and Learn more about the players that make up the team

Home Arena

Team Description

Unscramble the names of the baseball greats and test your knowledge of the sport

RITSAHINC LEICHY

- - - - - - - - - - - - - - - - - -

AXLE RIGDEUORZ

- - - - - - - - - - - - - - - - - -

AIDVD REIPC

- - - - - - - - - - - - - - - - - -

KNAH NERAA

- - - - - - - - - - - - - - - - - -

CABOJ MORGED

- - - - - - - - - - - - - - - - - -

HSOJ NANDLDOS

- - - - - - - - - - - - - - - - - -

Guess The Player #2

Put your skills to the test!
Can you identify the player from the clues given?

1. He has won numerous MVP awards and is widely regarded as one of the most talented players in modern baseball.

2. He has been a consistent All-Star selection and has helped lead his team to several playoff appearances.

3. He wears jersey number 27

4. He made his debut in 2011 and quickly became one of the league's brightest stars

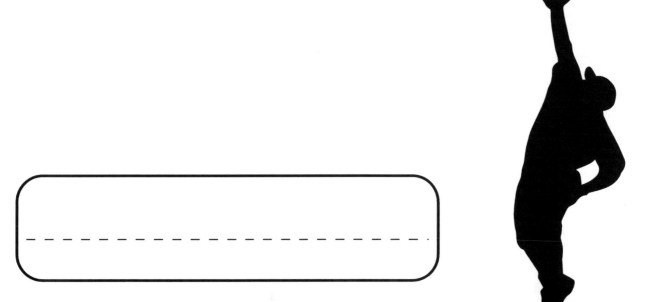

Baseball Glove Design

Get ready to unleash your creativity and design your very own baseball glove!

Baseball Math #2

Show off your math skills! Help the batter hit the ball out of the park and achieving an amazing home run by coloring only the circles that contain even numbers inside!

54 x 5 =

37 x 3 =

85 x 7 =

53 x 9 =

26 x 6 =

86 x 9 =

48 x 2 =

27 x 7 =

87 x 3 =

79 x 5 =

37 x 8 =

88 x 7 =

75 x 6 =

64 x 4 =

98 x 3 =

96 x 5 =

47 x 9 =

Crossword Game #2

Down

1. The act of a runner advancing to the next base without a defensive player forcing them out.

3. The fielding position between second and third base.

4. This happens when 4 balls are thrown in an at bat

5. The area where the players warm up before the game and during breaks.

6. The player who catches the pitches thrown by the pitcher.

8. The area where the pitcher throws the ball from.

Across

2. most common pitch to throw

7. The action of swinging and missing the ball three times, resulting in an out.

9. A hit that allows the batter to circle all the bases and score a run.

10. The term for a ball hit high into the air, giving fielders time to catch it.

Acrostic Poem #2

An acrostic poem is a type of poem where the first letter of each line spells out a word or phrase. All lines should relate to or Describe the poem.
Write an acrostic poem for the word below

PITCHER

P _____

i _____

T _____

C _____

H _____

E _____

R _____

Fun Baseball Facts

Jackie Robinson broke the color barrier in Major League Baseball in 1947 when he became the first African American player in the modern era.

Did You Know?

The distance from the pitcher's mound to home plate is 60 feet, 6 inches, which has been the standard distance since 1893.

The baseball glove was first introduced in the late 19th century to protect players hands from injuries when catching the ball.

The most amazing record for hitting home runs in a single season is 73!
Can you believe it? This incredible milestone was reached back in 2001

Connect the Dots #2

Join the fun! Connect the dots from 1 to 45 and discover the hidden picture

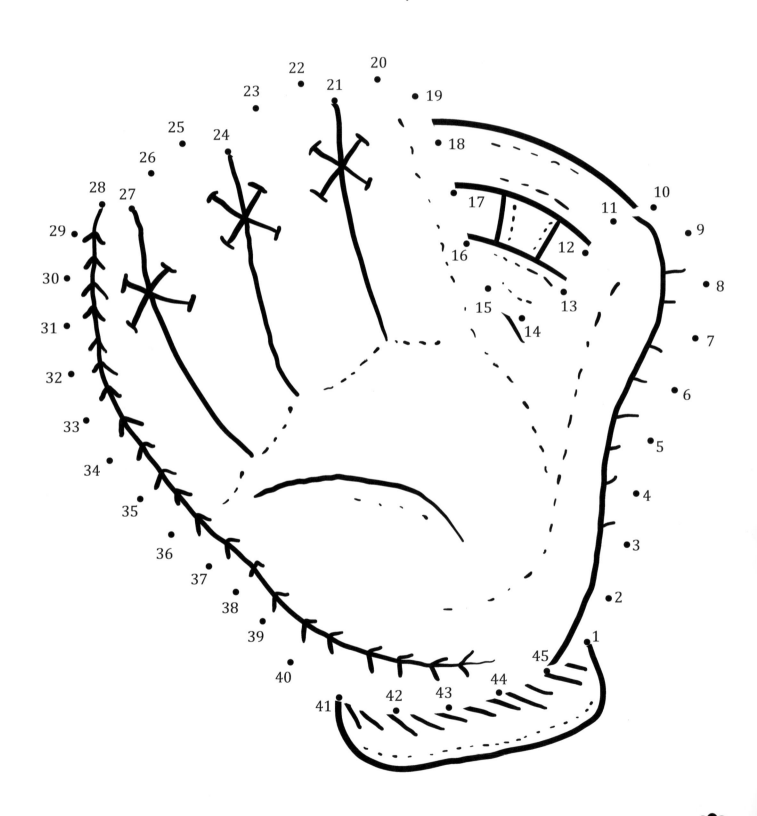

Capture the Fans' Emotions

The crowd goes wild as the team wins! Draw
a fan's face showing the excitement and joy of the moment

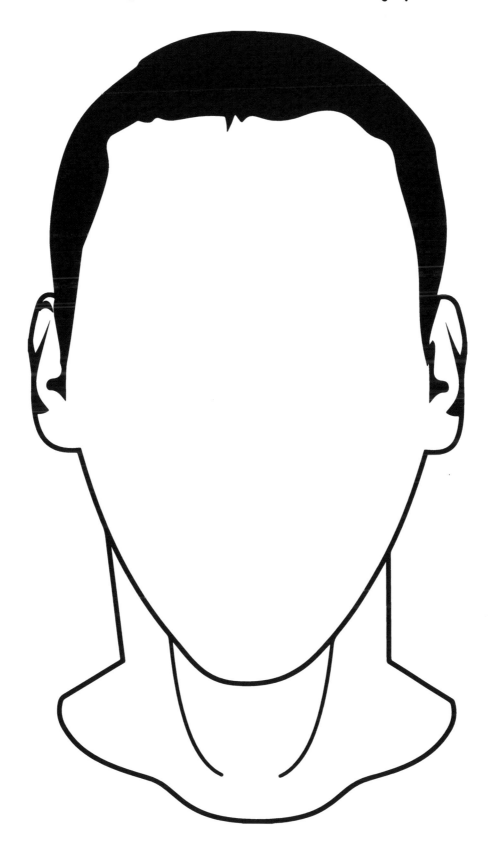

Drawing Activity

Put your artistic talents to use by replicating the image with your own drawing skills

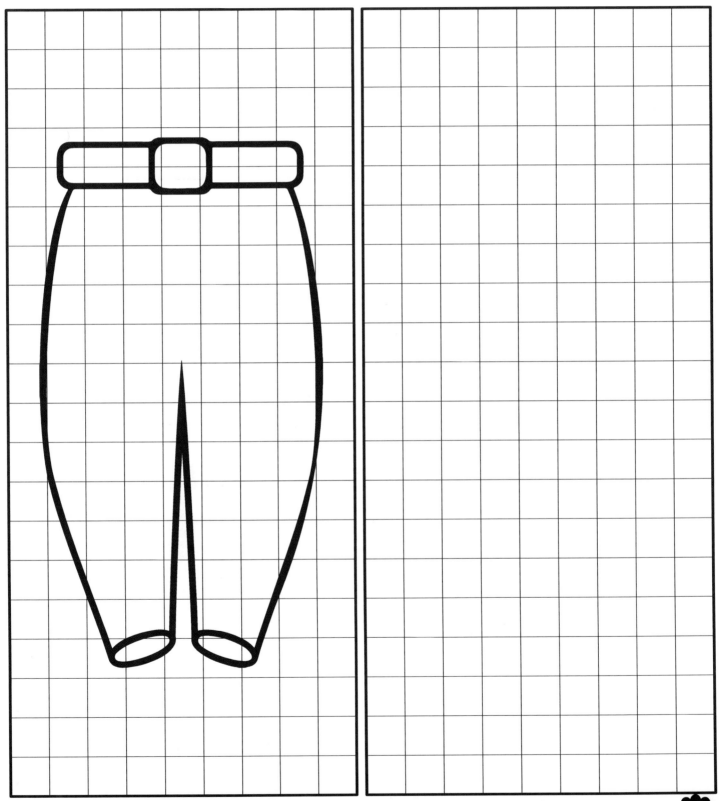

A To Z Players Names

Put your baseball knowledge to the test! Name your
Favorite players for each letter of the alphabet

A _____   B _____

C _____   D _____

E _____   F _____

G _____   H _____

I _____   J _____

K _____   L _____

M _____   N _____

O _____   P _____

Q _____   R _____

S _____   T _____

U _____   V _____

W _____   X _____

Y _____   Z _____

Baseball Scramble Game #2

Look at the letters around the picture.
Try to rearrange them to fill in the blanks

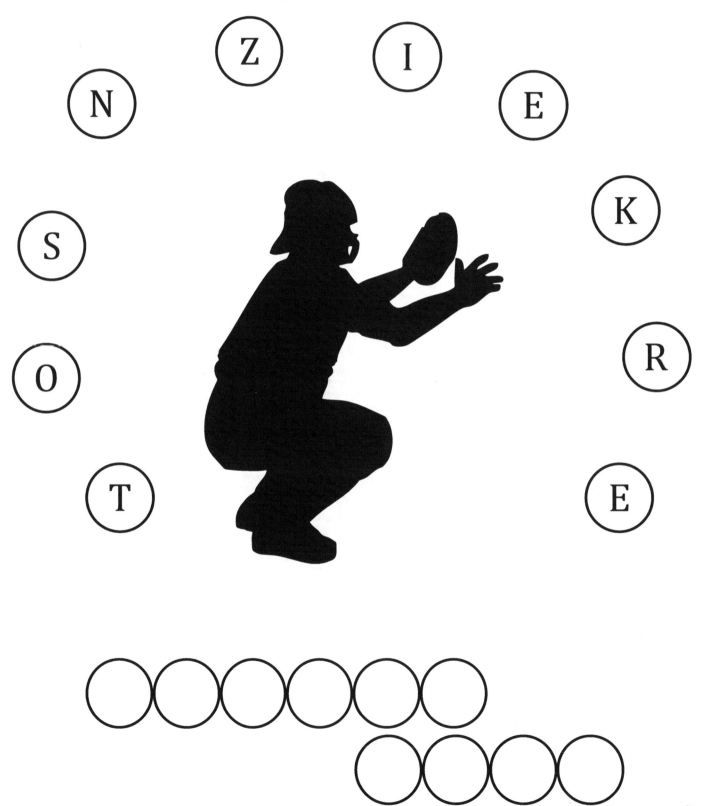

Baseball Math #3

Batter up! Step up to the plate, swing for the fences, and solve these multiplication problems and you'll be an All-Star in no time!

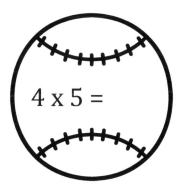 4 x 5 =

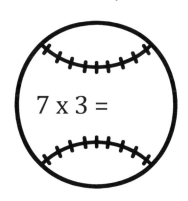 7 x 3 =

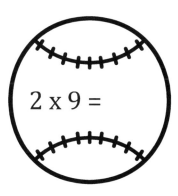 2 x 9 =

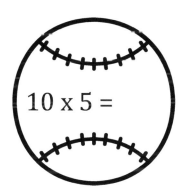 10 x 5 =

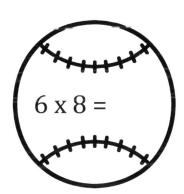 6 x 8 =

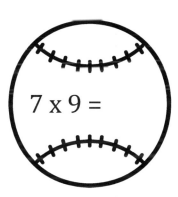 7 x 9 =

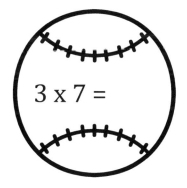 3 x 7 =

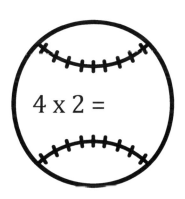 4 x 2 =

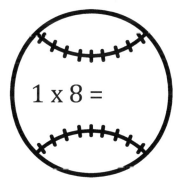 1 x 8 =

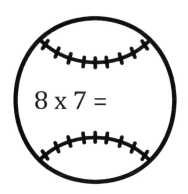 8 x 7 =

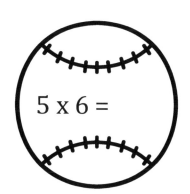 5 x 6 =

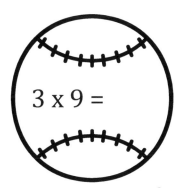 3 x 9 =

Baseball Commentary

Imagine you're a super cool announcer for a thrilling baseball game! Use exciting and vivid words to describe all the amazing things the players are doing on the field.
Get ready to add tons of excitement to your commentary!

Pitching Challenge!

Join forces with the pitcher and help them deliver an epic ball to the awaiting batter

Decoding Baseball Jokes #3

Can you solve the secret code and uncover the hidden answer

a	b	c	d	e	f	g	h	i	j	k	l	m
1	2	3	4	5	6	7	8	9	10	11	12	13

n	o	p	q	r	s	t	u	v	w	x	y	z
14	15	16	17	18	19	20	21	22	23	24	25	26

What's a baseball player's favorite dessert?

16	15	16	6	12	25

Why did the baseball coach bring a traffic light to the game?

20	15	19	5	14	4	19	9	7	14	1	12	19

What did home plate say about the ball?

9	20	19	16	15	9	14	20	12	5	19	19

What has 18 legs and catches flies?

1	2	1	19	5	2	1	12	12	20	5	1	13

Word Search #4

Uncovering the hidden baseball terms in the grid by looking in all directions, including backwards and diagonally

```
O T R I P L E P L A Y C A R T
Z N H X I Z R K W D B H L F A
V S Q M N N G O X H O U H C V
S T R A C U T G I K N Y N R W
P I T C H I N G M O U N D T Z
B O R A H A E C P N S C O T D
W R Z A I V D Y R E C M R Y R
L F S U T A G R G C N I Q O H
X T D S T R I K E Z O N E G Z
Y G A D E M I S O Y V A S B J
K O N I R P O P U P F K C D H
A H X M F O U L L I N E P H N
P I N C H R U N N E R B K T X
C E N T E R F I E L D E R K V
K F E G R V F T Q T Y Y F D Y
```

Pitching mound   Foul line   Pop-up

Center fielder   Triple   Bunt

Triple play   Pinch hitter   Tag

Strike zone   Pinch runner   Coach

Players Anagram Challenge #3

Unscramble the names of the baseball greats and test your knowledge of the sport

DET SWMLALII

- -

KCAZK GENRIEK

- -

YRRAB SNDOB

- -

GORER CLEMENS

- -

YECRB REPHAR

- -

GIELUM ABREACR

- -

Drawing Activity

Mirror the image! Finish the right side of the picture by copying the lines from the left side

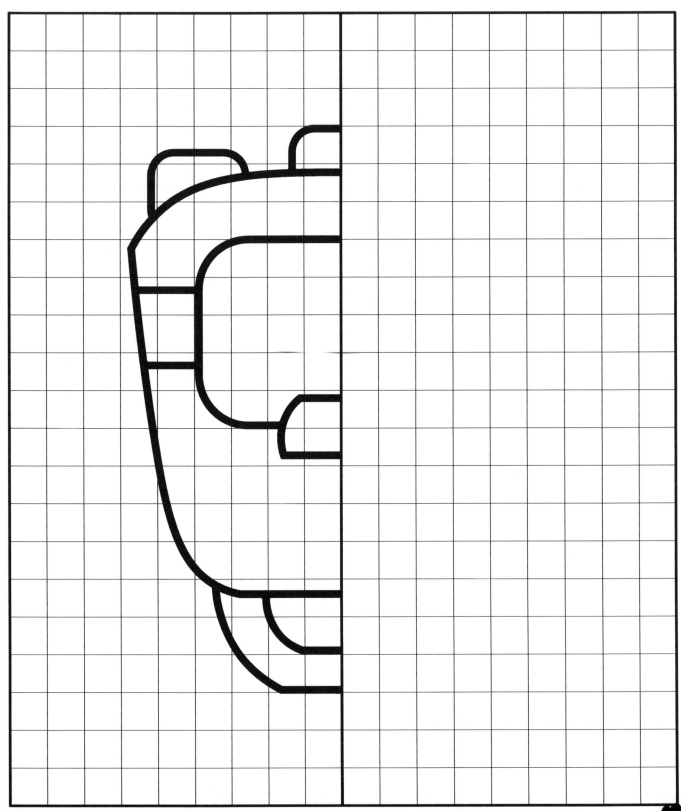

Fan Mail to the Pros

Pen a Letter to Your Favorite baseball player!
Share your thoughts and appreciation for your favorite player!

Dear, _____

_____
_____
_____
_____
_____
_____
_____
_____
_____
_____
_____
_____
_____
_____
_____

Love _____

Baseball Ball Design

Get ready to unleash your creativity and design your very own baseball Ball!

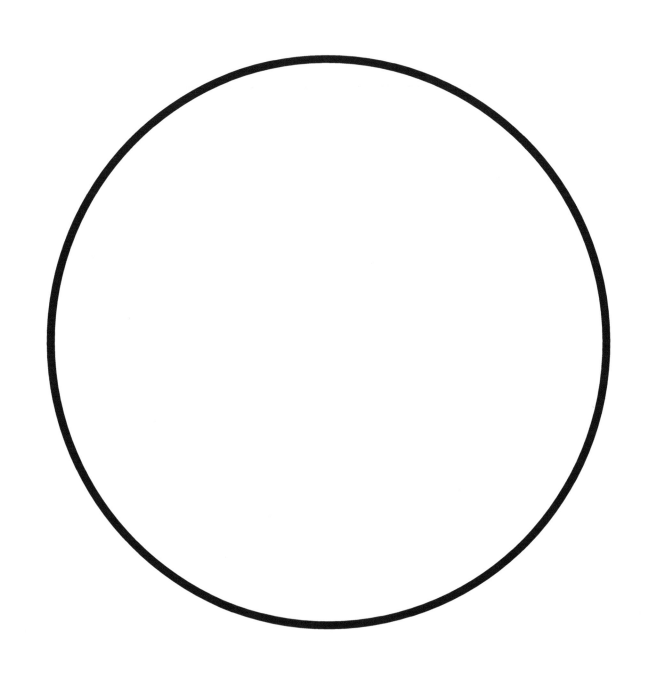

Guess The Player #3

Put your skills to the test!
Can you identify the player from the clues given?

1. This player is known for his powerful hitting and has hit over 600 career home runs

2. This player has been named the MVP of the National League three times

3. This player is originally from the Dominican Republic and has represented his country in international competitions

4. This player has achieved numerous career milestones, including reaching 3,000 hits.

Crossword Game #3

Across

3. Pitch that goes down the middle

4. The area where the players warm up before entering the game.

6. Shape of a baseball field

7. The act of a baserunner advancing to the next base without a hit or an out.

10. Pitch that changes speed

Down

1. Ball that rolls on the ground

2. Name of the white squares the players run to

5. Ball that is driectly at you

8. When you are next up to bat you are...

9. When you hit and you run to first base

Acrostic Poem #3

An acrostic poem is a type of poem where the first letter of each line spells out a word or phrase. All lines should relate to or Describe the poem.
Write an acrostic poem for the word below

HOME RUN

H _____

O _____

M _____

E _____

R _____

U _____

N _____

Fun Baseball Facts

Did You Know?

Pitchers are super strong and can throw baseballs really, really fast! Some of them can even throw the ball faster than 100 miles per hour!

Most baseball games last around three hours, but did you know that one game in 1910 was super speedy? It finished in just over half an hour, making it one of the fastest games ever played!

Did you know that hotdogs are the all-time favorite food at baseball games? They're super popular!

Baseballs are made with cork or rubber inside and covered in leather. The cork or rubber helps the ball bounce, and the leather keeps it in shape. That's why baseballs are great for throwing, holding, and hitting

Baseball Math #4

Hit a home run by solving these two-digit addition problems, using regrouping if needed

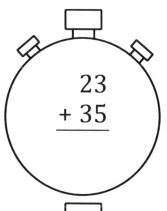
23
+ 35

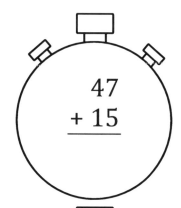
47
+ 15

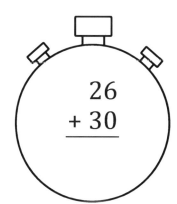
26
+ 30

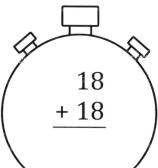
18
+ 18

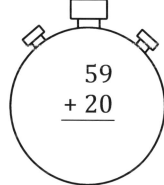
59
+ 20

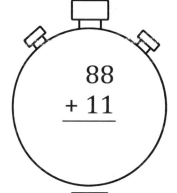
88
+ 11

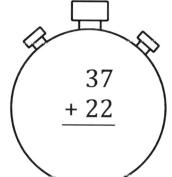
37
+ 22

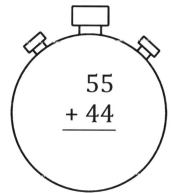
55
+ 44

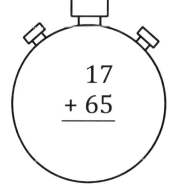
17
+ 65

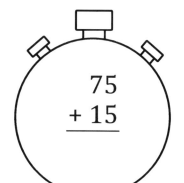
75
+ 15

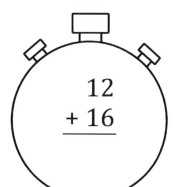
12
+ 16

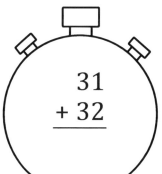
31
+ 32

Rivalry Research

Scout out the competition! Research one of the teams that will be facing off against your favorite team this season

Team Information

Team Name: _ _ _ _ _ _ _ _ _ _ _ _ _ _ _

Nickname: _ _ _ _ _ _ _ _ _ _ _ _ _ _

Location: _ _ _ _ _ _ _ _ _ _ _ _ _ _

Coach: _ _ _ _ _ _ _ _ _ _ _ _ _ _ _

Stadium: _ _ _ _ _ _ _ _ _ _ _ _ _ _

History: _ _ _ _ _ _ _ _ _ _ _ _ _ _

_ _ _ _ _ _ _ _ _ _ _ _ _ _ _ _

_ _ _ _ _ _ _ _ _ _ _ _ _ _ _ _

_ _ _ _ _ _ _ _ _ _ _ _ _ _ _ _

_ _ _ _ _ _ _ _ _ _ _ _ _ _ _ _

Head-to-Head Matchups

This season: _ _ _ _ _ _ _ _ _ _ _ _

_ _ _ _ _ _ _ _ _ _ _ _ _ _ _ _

All-time: _ _ _ _ _ _ _ _ _ _ _ _ _

_ _ _ _ _ _ _ _ _ _ _ _ _ _ _ _

Predict the outcome of the game and Guess the MVP of the game

_ _ _ _ _ _ _ _ _ _ _ _ _ _ _ _

_ _ _ _ _ _ _ _ _ _ _ _ _ _ _ _

_ _ _ _ _ _ _ _ _ _ _ _ _ _ _ _

_ _ _ _ _ _ _ _ _ _ _ _ _ _ _ _

_ _ _ _ _ _ _ _ _ _ _ _ _ _ _ _

_ _ _ _ _ _ _ _ _ _ _ _ _ _ _ _

Team Statistics

Batting Statistics: _ _ _ _ _ _ _ _ _ _

_ _ _ _ _ _ _ _ _ _ _ _ _ _ _ _

Pitching Statistics: _ _ _ _ _ _ _ _ _ _

_ _ _ _ _ _ _ _ _ _ _ _ _ _ _ _

Defensive Statistics: _ _ _ _ _ _ _ _ _

_ _ _ _ _ _ _ _ _ _ _ _ _ _ _ _

Team Strategy

Style of Play: _ _ _ _ _ _ _ _ _ _ _ _

_ _ _ _ _ _ _ _ _ _ _ _ _ _ _ _

_ _ _ _ _ _ _ _ _ _ _ _ _ _ _ _

_ _ _ _ _ _ _ _ _ _ _ _ _ _ _ _

_ _ _ _ _ _ _ _ _ _ _ _ _ _ _ _

Strengths: _ _ _ _ _ _ _ _ _ _ _ _ _

_ _ _ _ _ _ _ _ _ _ _ _ _ _ _ _

_ _ _ _ _ _ _ _ _ _ _ _ _ _ _ _

_ _ _ _ _ _ _ _ _ _ _ _ _ _ _ _

_ _ _ _ _ _ _ _ _ _ _ _ _ _ _ _

Weaknesses: _ _ _ _ _ _ _ _ _ _ _

_ _ _ _ _ _ _ _ _ _ _ _ _ _ _ _

_ _ _ _ _ _ _ _ _ _ _ _ _ _ _ _

_ _ _ _ _ _ _ _ _ _ _ _ _ _ _ _

_ _ _ _ _ _ _ _ _ _ _ _ _ _ _ _

Key Players to Watch Out For: _ _ _ _

_ _ _ _ _ _ _ _ _ _ _ _ _ _ _ _

_ _ _ _ _ _ _ _ _ _ _ _ _ _ _ _

_ _ _ _ _ _ _ _ _ _ _ _ _ _ _ _

_ _ _ _ _ _ _ _ _ _ _ _ _ _ _ _

Connect the Dots #3

Join the fun! Connect the dots from 1 to 45 and discover
the hidden picture

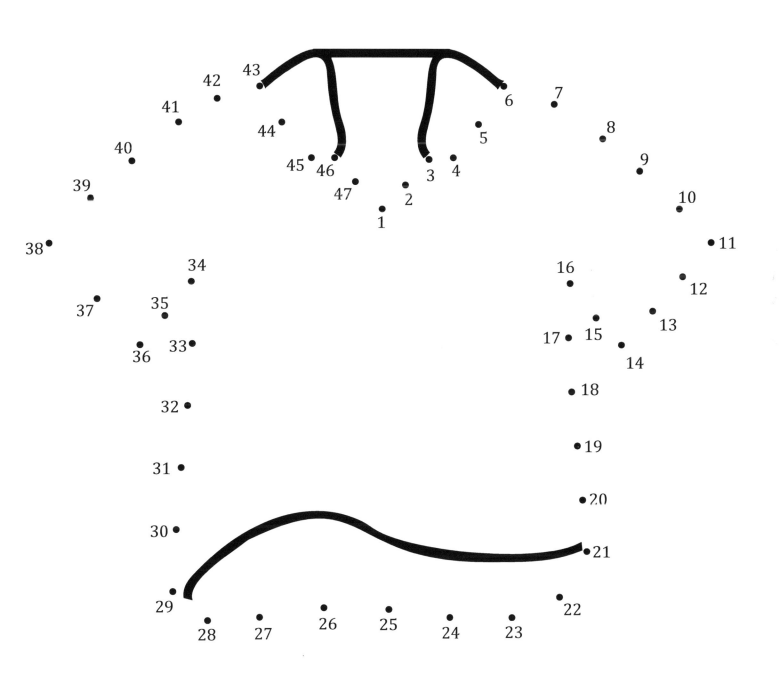

Baseball Journaling

Step up to the plate, grab your pen, and express your love for baseball

What is your favorite thing about playing baseball?

What is your favorite baseball memory?

What are the qualities that make a great baseball player?

Baseball Bat Design

Get ready to unleash your creativity and design your very
own baseball Bat!

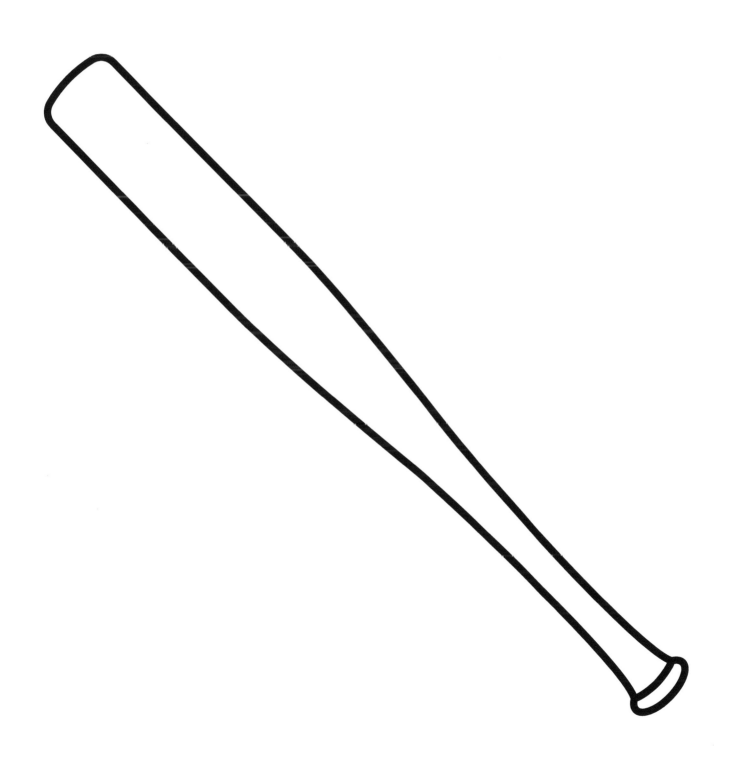

Baseball Scramble Game #3

Look at the letters around the picture.
Try to rearrange them to fill in the blanks

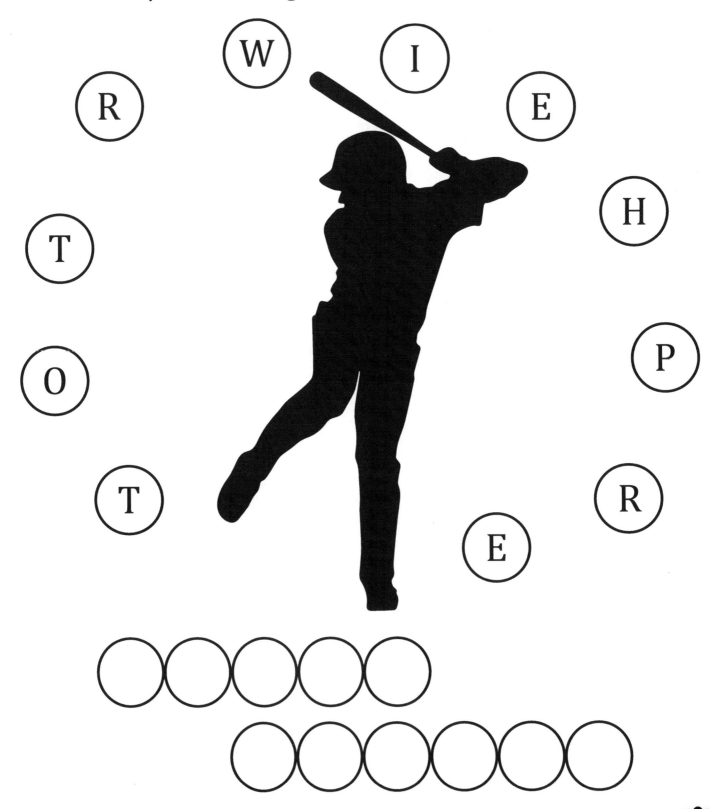

Decoding Baseball Jokes #4

Can you solve the secret code and uncover the hidden answer

a	b	c	d	e	f	g	h	i	j	k	l	m
1	2	3	4	5	6	7	8	9	10	11	12	13

n	o	p	q	r	s	t	u	v	w	x	y	z
14	15	16	17	18	19	20	21	22	23	24	25	26

Which animal is best at hitting a baseball?

20	8	5	2	1	20

What do you get when you cross a tree with a baseball player?

2	1	2	5	18	15	15	20

What type of baseball do they play in England?

20	5	1	2	1	12	12

What is a baseball player's favorite thing about going to the park?

20	8	5	19	23	9	14	7	19

Word Search #5

Uncovering the hidden baseball terms in the grid by looking in all directions, including backwards and diagonally

```
W U E P S C Q N Y T W F K P F
F O A N F L E K E O U S I A I
B A T T I N G A V E R A G E E
U S A C R I F I C E F L Y A L
C M P G S W S N Y I Z Z O G D
N P B A T T I N G O R D E R E
J L A L B C E H P P E Y M O R
W Q T Y A H R G J V D X J U S
B V T N S A W H I H U Y N N C
X R E Q E N R R O P G M P D H
W P R S M G D F I H O E S B O
E L A D A E A S Q X U P A A I
H B O L N U P X T A T S F L C
B E M I Q P K Y Z G Y K A L E
B C L A A P F I Q C S H O I Y
```

Fielder's choice   Ground ball   Base

Sacrifice fly   Line drive   Batter

First baseman   Changeup   Pop fly

Batting average   Batting order   Dugout

In 20 Years...

Imagine yourself 20 years in the future, as a professional baseball player! Complete the sentences below to share your dreams and goals. Fill in the blanks with your ideas and dreams. Have fun dreaming big and let your imagination soar!

By: _____

When I step onto the baseball field, I will be known as _____.

My position on the team will be _____, where I will excel at _____.

I will be playing for the _____ team, known for their _____.

I will have won _____ championships with my team, showcasing our dedication and teamwork.

In my first season, I will break the record for _____, leaving fans in awe.

As a baseball player, I will inspire others with my _____ _____and _____.

Off the field, I will be involved in _____, using my platform to make a positive impact.

My signature move on the field will be _____, surprising opponents and thrilling fans.

When I'm not playing, I will spend my time _____, always seeking ways to improve my skills.

Tattoo Design

If your favorite baseball player has a tattoo, what do you think it would be of? Draw and color a tattoo design for your your favorite baseball player!

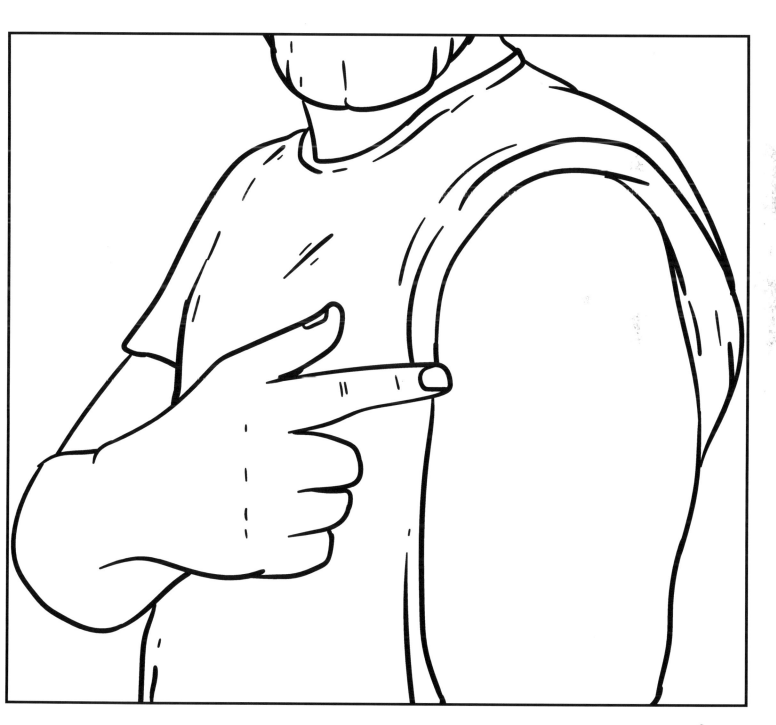

Home Run Maze

Navigate through the maze and guide the player to hit the ball and score an incredible home run!

Baseball Math #5

Use the numbers on the trophy to fill in the
circles and complete the multiplication equations

$\bigcirc$ x $\bigcirc$ = 10

$\bigcirc$ x $\bigcirc$ = 10

$\bigcirc$ x $\bigcirc$ = 12

$\bigcirc$ x $\bigcirc$ = 12

$\bigcirc$ x $\bigcirc$ = 16

$\bigcirc$ x $\bigcirc$ = 16

Unscramble the names of the baseball greats and test your knowledge of the sport

XAM REZSCHER

- -

NOHTYWAH SALYAHCREK

- -

AESM SULAIM

- -

EOYJ TVTO

- -

ROGER CLEMENS

- -

EMOKIO TSEB

- -

Baseball Cleats Design

Get ready to unleash your creativity and design your very own Baseball Cleats!

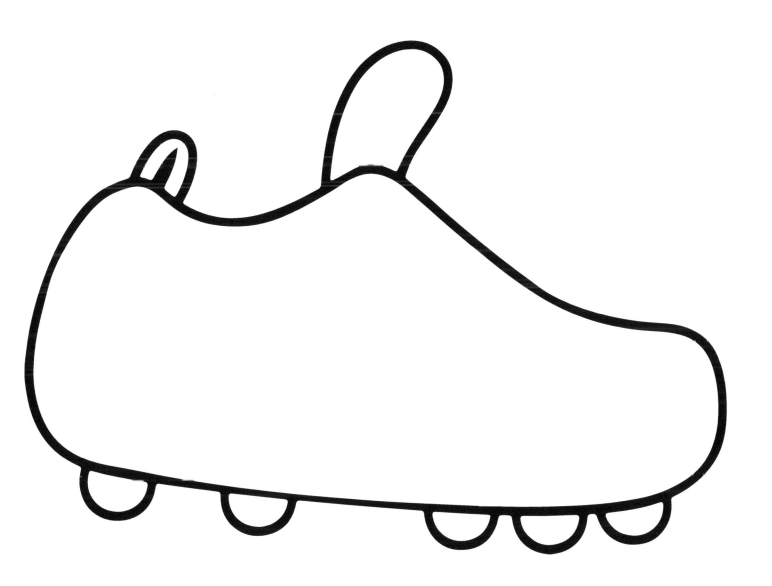

Drawing Activity

Put your artistic talents to use by replicating the image with your own drawing skills

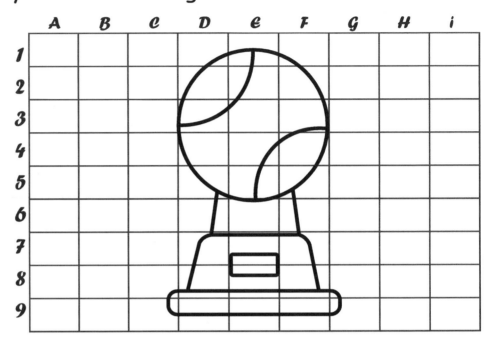

Baseball Scramble Game #4

Look at the letters around the picture.
Try to rearrange them to fill in the blanks

Baseball Smoothie Creation

Players need lots of energy to fuel their powerful performances on the field! Get creative and make a nutritious, baseball-inspired smoothie to keep you energized for the game. Decorate your cup and showcase your unique creation!

Name of the Smoothie: _____

Ingredients Needed:

_____

_____

_____

_____

_____

_____

_____

_____

_____

_____

_____

Solutions

Word Search #1

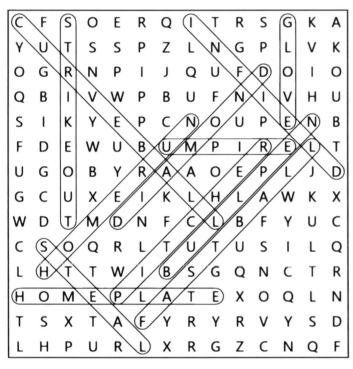

Pitching Challenge Maze

Math Meets Maze

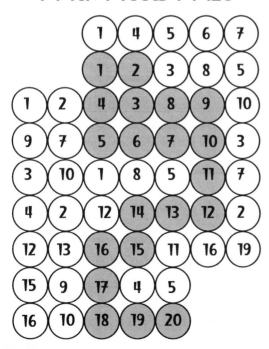

Decoding Baseball Jokes #1

Q. Where does a baseball player go when he needs a new uniform?

A. New Jersey

Q. Where should a baseball player never wear red?

A. In the bull pen

Q. What do baseball players eat on?

A. Home plates

Word Search #2

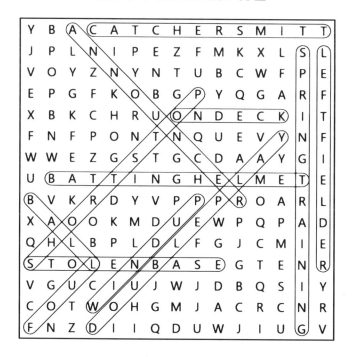

Strike for Glory

Acrostic Poem #1

(possible answer)

Bouncing balls and bats in hand,

Athletes running across the sand.

Swinging, catching, throwing too,

Everyone loves this game, it's true!

Big crowds cheering, excitement in the air,

All united by this sport we share.

Let's play together, have some fun,

Leaping and sliding under the sun!

Crossword Game #1

```
        ¹f
  ²t    u
   r    l        ³o
   i    l         u
   p    c          t
⁵f l y  o  u  t    s
   e    u          s
        n
                        ⁴s                ⁶p
                         e                 i
                         c                 t
                         o                 c
      ⁷s t r i k e z o n  e                 h
                         d                 e
                         b                         ⁸g
               ⁹b a s e r u n  n  e  r              r
                         s                         a
      ¹⁰d o u b l e                                 n
                         m                         d
                         a                         s
                         n                         l
                                                   a
                                                   m
```

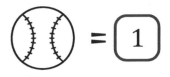

🧢 = 1

🧤 = 2

⛑ = 4

🏏 = 3

Baseball Scramble Game #1

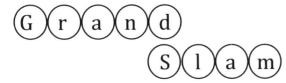

G r a n d
S l a m

The Lost Bat

Decoding Baseball Jokes #2

Q. Why was the baseball player at the store?

A. For a sales pitch

Q. What did the baseball glove say to the ball?

A. Catch you later

Q. What do you call a baseball player who doesn't take a bath?

A. A dirty slider

Q. What's a baseball player's favorite type of music?

A. Swing

Word Search #3

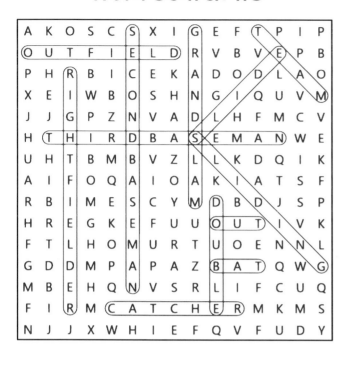

Baseball Math #1

54 x 5 =   37 x 3 =   85 x 7 =

53 x 9 =   26 x 6 =   86 x 9 =   48 x 2 =

27 x 7 =   87 x 3 =   79 x 5 =   37 x 8 =

88 x 7 =   75 x 6 =   64 x 4 =   98 x 3 =

96 x 5 =   47 x 9 =

Crossword Game #2

Acrostic Poem #2
(possible answer)

Powerful throws with all their might,

Intense focus, aiming just right.

Taking charge on that pitcher's mound,

Commanding the game with every sound.

Handling pressure, delivering their best,

Every pitch puts them to the test.

Reliable and strong, they lead the way,

Baseball Scramble Game #2

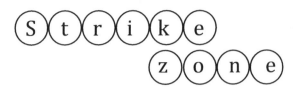

Baseball Math #3

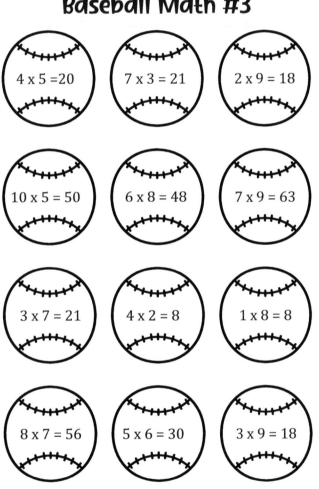

Pitching Challenge!

Decoding Baseball Jokes #3

Q. What's a baseball player's favorite dessert?

A. Pop "fly"

Q: Why did the baseball coach bring a traffic light to the game?

A: To send signals

Q: What did home plate say about the ball?

A: It's pointless

Q: What has 18 legs and catches flies?

A: A baseball team

Word Search #4

```
O T R I P L E P L A Y C A R T
Z N H X I Z R K W D B H L F A
V S Q M N N G O X H O U H C V
S T R A C U T G I K N Y N R W
P I T C H I N G M O U N D T Z
B O R A H A E C P N S C O T D
W R Z A I V D Y R E C M R Y R
L F S U T A G R G C N I Q O H
X T D S T R I K E Z O N E G Z
Y G A D E M I S O Y V A S B J
K O N I R P O P U P F K C D H
A H X M F O U L L I N E P H N
P I N C H R U N N E R B K T X
C E N T E R F I E L D E R K V
K F E G R V F T Q T Y Y F D Y
```

Crossword Game #3

Acrostic Poem #3
(possible answer)

Hitting with power, the ball takes flight,
Out of the park, a magnificent sight.
Making circles around the bases with glee,
Everyone rises, clapping with jubilee.
Roaring cheers fill the stadium's air,
Unleashing joy and excitement rare.
Nailing that swing, a perfect connection,

Baseball Scramble Game #3

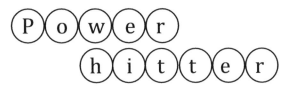

Decoding Baseball Jokes #4

Q: Which animal is best at hitting a baseball?

A: The bat.

Q: What do you get when you cross a tree with a baseball player?

A: Babe Root.

Q: What type of baseball do they play in England?

A: Tea Ball.

Q: What is a baseball player's favorite thing about going to the park?

A: The swings.

Baseball Math #4

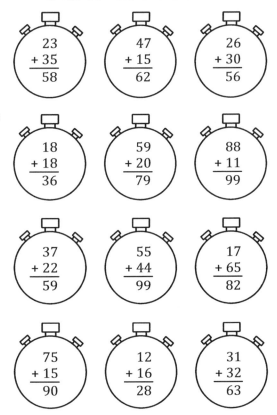

23 + 35 = 58	47 + 15 = 62	26 + 30 = 56
18 + 18 = 36	59 + 20 = 79	88 + 11 = 99
37 + 22 = 59	55 + 44 = 99	17 + 65 = 82
75 + 15 = 90	12 + 16 = 28	31 + 32 = 63

Word Search #5

```
W U E P S C Q N Y T W F K P F
F O A N F L E K E O U S I A I
B A T T I N G A V E R A G E E
U S A C R I F I C E F L Y A L
C M P G S W S N Y I Z Z O G D
N P B A T T I N G O R D E R E
J L A L B C E H P P E Y M O R
W Q T Y A H R G J V D X J U S
B V T N S A W H I H U Y N N C
X R E Q E N R R O P G M P D H
W P R S M G D F I H O E S B O
E L A D A E A S Q X U P A A I
H B O L N U P X T A T S F L C
B E M I Q P K Y Z G Y K A L E
B C L A A P F I Q C S H O I Y
```

Home Run Maze

Baseball Math #5

10	x	1	=	10
5	x	2	=	10
6	x	2	=	12
3	x	4	=	12
8	x	2	=	16
4	x	4	=	16

Baseball Scramble Game #4

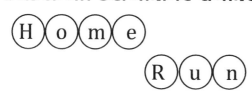

H o m e

R u n

Thank you for purchasing our activity book for kids!

We hope your child had fun completing the activities and that the book brought a little bit of fun and creativity into their day.

If you have a moment, we would really appreciate it if you could leave a review on Amazon. Your feedback helps other parents decide if the book is right for their children, and it helps us improve and reach more families in need of educational and entertaining resources. Plus, it's always nice to hear what people think of our work!

Thank you in advance for your help, and we hope you and your child have a great day!

Kindest regards,

Creative Funland

Made in the USA
Las Vegas, NV
16 July 2024